P9-BTM-249

animals**animals**

Foxes

by **Marc Tyler Nobleman**

mc **Marshall Cavendish**
Benchmark
New York

Thanks to John Behler for his expert reading of this manuscript.

Marshall Cavendish Benchmark
99 White Plains Road
Tarrytown, New York 10591-9001
www.marshallcavendish.us

All Internet sites were available and accurate when sent to press.

Library of Congress Cataloging-in-Publication Data
Nobleman, Marc Tyler.
Foxes / by Marc Tyler Nobleman.
p. cm.—(Animals, animals)
Summary: "Describes the physical characteristics, behavior, habitat, and endangered status of foxes"—
Provided by publisher.
Includes bibliographical references and index.
ISBN-13: 978-0-7614-2237-2
ISBN-10: 0-7614-2237-4
1. Foxes—Juvenile literature. I. Title. II. Series.
QL737.C22N63 2006
599.775—dc22 2005025608

Photo research by Joan Meisel

Cover photo: Mark Hamblin/WWl/Peter Arnold, Inc.

The photographs in this book are used by permission and through the courtesy of:
Animals Animals: 1, Norbert Rosing; 4, Peter Weimann; 6, R. Toms/OSF;
7, Darren Bennett; 8, Rick Edwards; 9, 28, Daniel A. Bedell; 10, O.
Newman/OSF; 12, Joe McDonald; 18, Leonard Rue; 20, 24, Phyllis
Greenberg; 22, 36, Irwin & Peggy Bauer; 23, Jack Wilburn; 26, 34,
Momatiuk/Eastcott; 30, Dominique Braud; 33, Jennifer Loomis; 35, Alain
Dragesco-Joffel; 37, D & J Bartlett/OSF; 38, J. Stachecki; 41, Ralph
Reinhold; Peter Arnold, Inc.: 14, Wildwood/Paul Glendell; 32, Tom Vezo;
Photo Researchers, Inc.: 16, Adam Jones;

Editor: Mary Perrotta Rich
Editorial Director: Michelle Bisson
Art Director: Anahid Hamparian
Series Designer: Adam Mietlowski

Printed in Malaysia

3 5 6 4 2

Contents

1 Introducing Foxes

Early on a foggy morning, a red fox searches for food on the border of a field and a forest. Suddenly it hears a rustle. Then it glimpses movement across the grass. Something is approaching rapidly. The fox's heart begins to race—and so does the fox. It darts into the forest. Within seconds, more than a dozen foxhounds—dogs that humans *breed* to hunt foxes—are chasing it through the trees, barking. The fox dashes around shrubs and leaps over fallen logs. Humans on horseback are shouting at the dogs to run faster. The fox spots a small hole up ahead and dives in. It scrambles as deep into the ground as it can. The panting dogs

A red fox is capable of leaping over a stream—a good skill to have when being chased by foxhounds.

Horses and hounds await the beginning of a foxhunt in the United Kingdom.

try to get at the fox, but after a few moments of pawing the earth, they give up. The dogs and people leave. The fox has saved itself.

This foxhunt ended as many do—with the fox escaping. However, the sport of foxhunting would not have lasted for as many centuries as it has if every fox

6

escaped. When foxhounds do catch a fox, they surround and kill it. For many years, many people have condemned foxhunting as a cruel sport. In 2004 foxhunting using hounds was banned in parts of its traditional home, the United Kingdom, amid both cheers and protests.

Foxes are the smallest members of the Canidae family, which also includes wolves, coyotes, jackals,

A coyote belongs to the dog family, as does the fox.

and *domestic* dogs. Foxes are among the most wide-spread and adaptable mammals in the world, living in environments ranging from desert to *tundra*. The best known—the red and the gray fox—prefer habitats that border two types of landscape, such as forest and fields. That gives them a greater choice of and chance for capturing *prey*.

Two black-backed jackals play with a beetle.

It's amazing that this red fox does not break the kittiwake egg it is holding.

Foxes are *omnivores* that are most active at night, dawn, and dusk. Their diet varies depending on the region in which they live, but they eat small mammals, particularly mice and rabbits, as well as insects. They will eat birds and eggs, though they do not raid

This arctic fox is burying a snow goose egg in the summer while food is plentiful.

henhouses as regularly as folktales suggest. In general, foxes avoid noisy prey such as farm fowl. Yet, even though they only occasionally steal chickens, and actually reduce the population of more destructive pests such as rodents that eat crops, some farmers consider foxes to be pests. They will also eat *carrion* since it takes less energy to acquire than hunting for fresh meat does.

If foxes find themselves with more food than they can eat, they will *cache* the leftovers, or bury them under leaves or dirt. They remember the hiding places and return for the food another day. Their secret stash is especially valuable during winter or periods of food shortages. Although they spread out their supply and hide it well, other animals do sometimes find foxes' caches.

One of Aesop's fables famously tells of a fox that sees a crow with a piece of meat in its beak sitting in a tree. Hungry, the fox wonders aloud if the crow's voice is as attractive as its appearance. To prove that it is, the crow opens its beak and lets out a *caw!* The meat drops and the fox retrieves it, just as he planned.

Of course real foxes cannot use tricks like that, but they are intelligent animals. Outsmarting a group of

Perhaps it is the expression on this gray fox's face that makes people think foxes are sly or mischievous.

foxhounds that greatly outnumbers them demonstrates this. Foxes are not deceptive or sly, as they are sometimes characterized. They simply have a good survival instinct that they are skilled at following.

In fact, a fox is more likely to be wary and shy. Unlike most canines that travel in families or packs, foxes are *solitary*, except when they are breeding. Like many woodland animals, they would rather avoid people. Yet they can also be curious and develop a trust of humans, particularly if humans feed them. People have reported seeing foxes enjoying food left out for pets, most often dogs, alongside the pets themselves. Perhaps that is not so surprising, since dogs and foxes are related. But foxes are wild animals, and humans should not feed them. Some human food, including chocolate, may make foxes sick.

The average lifespan of a wild fox is three to five years, though some live up to ten years or more. Survival is naturally difficult, and some fox species are considered *endangered*. Humans are their most common *predators*, and they do not have many others. Coyotes, wolves, or large birds of prey may occasionally attack foxes. Tiny *parasites* called *mites* can irritate foxes, causing them to scratch their fur constantly. This may lead to *mange*, a condition that weakens and sometimes causes the death of foxes. Despite these threats, foxes continue to thrive.

Did You Know . . .

Rabies is a viral disease that regularly threatens the fox population worldwide. It is commonly spread when an infected animal bites another animal—even a human. Once symptoms develop, rabies is fast acting and almost always fatal. There is no known cure for rabies. Some countries try to prevent it by *vaccinating* wildlife, including foxes.

2 Fox Bodies

Though foxes can vary in size and color, they share certain features. The average adult fox is slightly larger than a house cat and can weigh up to 15 pounds (6.8 kilograms). Male foxes, called *dogs*, are usually bigger than females, called *vixens*.

Generally, foxes have pointed snouts, erect pointed ears, a thick coat of fur, slender legs, and bushy tails called *brushes*. A typical red fox is 36 to 42 inches (90 to 106 centimeters) in length, roughly a third of which is its tail (14 to 16 inches, or 35 to 40 centimeters). Because their tails are a substantial part of their total length, foxes can appear bigger than they really are. Red fox tails have white tips. Scientists are

See how long the fox's tail is compared to the length of its body?

It doesn't seem natural to see a fox in a tree, but here one is!

not sure why, but it may be to draw the attention of other foxes or to provide camouflage. Their legs and feet are black, and the tops of their ears are, too.

Foxes are canines that sometimes act like cats. Foxes do not run down prey like other canine predators. Instead, they sneak up and remain still until they can pounce. Sometimes they kill their prey instantly. Other times, they play with it by holding it down, letting it go, and giving chase again, or perhaps tossing it in the air and catching it. Also like cats, fox eyes have vertical pupils. The backs of their eyes have a *tapetum*, a reflective surface that creates more light and therefore improves their night vision. It makes their eyes glow in the dark the way cats' eyes do.

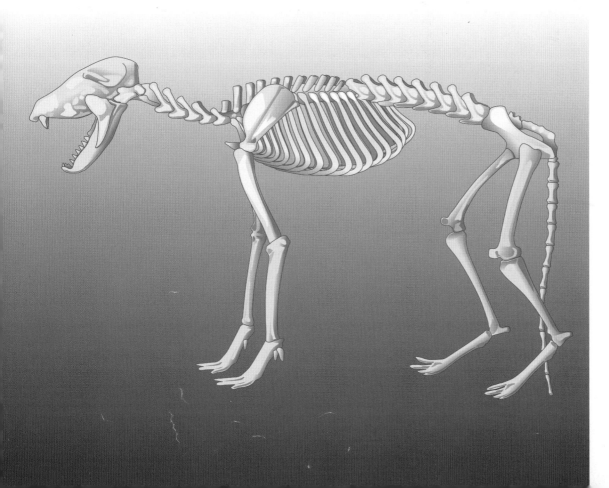

A fox seems much smaller when you see only its skeleton.

This red fox is enjoying a meal it detected with its powerful sense of smell.

Yet there is disagreement over whether foxes' eyesight is strong. Red foxes have better vision than other species have. In general, foxes' yellow eyes are designed to notice motion—even the twitch of a rabbit's ear—but if a creature stands still in a fox's line of sight, the fox might not see it.

However, a fox's sense of hearing and of smell are excellent. Unlike many mammals, foxes can detect low-frequency sounds such as scraping in dirt, made by some underground prey. Once they locate prey that way, they can pinpoint it precisely by smell and get to it quickly with their claws.

When in search of a meal, a fox knows that being silent is critical. Otherwise, foxes make a number of vocalizations when they are startled, signaling to mates, or warning other foxes of danger. At times they can sound like dogs, but they do have a high-pitched call all their own. They can also make yips, screams, and assorted growls.

Foxes can run up to 30 miles (48 kilometers) per hour. Running is not key to its hunting strategy, but after creeping up close to prey, a fox does need to sprint the final few feet to nab it. Plus, running does come in handy when foxes need to flee from danger.

3 The Fox Life Cycle

In winter, female red foxes leave scent signs for males indicating that they are ready to mate. Once mating occurs, the female is pregnant for about eight weeks. The parents-to-be establish a *den*—sometimes more than one. That way, if another animal invades or disturbs one of their dens, they immediately have others to go to.

Foxes do not build their dens but rather move into *burrows* that have been abandoned by other animals. Some dens may be in caves, dense brush, hollow logs, or spaces under large rocks, tree roots, or fallen trees. The den is lined with dry grass and leaves to protect the newborn foxes from damp ground.

A red fox kit peeks out of its den.

Did You Know . . .

Fox dens often have more than one entrance and exit so foxes have a better chance of escaping if that need arises.

A red fox vixen is returning to her den, where her two-month-old kits wait for her.

22

A den is primarily for birthing and then nurturing young foxes. Foxes do not live in dens during any other time of the year. Many of them sleep outdoors, concealed by grasses. They wrap their large tails around their bodies for warmth.

Close to the beginning of spring, the female red fox gives birth to a *litter* of one to ten gray or black *kits*. The average number of kits is four. Each enters the world weighing about 4 ounces (113.4 grams). Some

This red fox is bringing arctic ground squirrels back to its den to feed its pups.

These red fox kits are playing right outside the opening to their den.

will not survive their first year. Sometimes parents move the kits to another den for safety. Sometimes they move them for no obvious reason. If a potential predator gets near the den the kits are in, the father will try to lead the other animal away without a fight.

The first year of a fox's life is a period of dramatic growth. Kits are born blind and deaf, but that condition does not last long. Their vision develops in their second week, when they open their eyes for the first time, and their hearing at about the same time. Their mother remains with them in the den and feeds them with her milk while their father brings her food. At three weeks the kits begin to frolic, and their fur begins to change to whatever color it will eventually be. At five weeks, they start to nip at their parents' food. They also begin to explore the world beyond their den. If they wander too far, they may cry for their mother, who will guide them back to the den.

Little red foxes love to play with their siblings. They practice crouching and pouncing on one another. They may even catch an insect—their first prey. Soon their playfulness becomes competitive. After days of biting and chasing one another, one will emerge as the dominant kit and will then get to eat

Sometimes red fox kits play more aggressively, as these two are doing among the rocks in Alaska.

first. Afterward the kits become playmates again and gradually explore farther from the den. In summer all of them continue to sharpen their hunting skills by observing their mother, but they still rely on their parents for food.

Around five months, by which point autumn has arrived, the kits are nearly fully grown. Most will leave their mother to start their adult lives, though some females stay longer. The mother may snarl at the kits to get them to go. Winter brings longer nights, giving the foxes more time to hunt. And they need it: food is harder to come by in cold weather.

As they search for their own territories, red foxes may cover many miles. They are careful to avoid territories that other foxes have already claimed. Sometimes two foxes will clash over a territory. They will bare their teeth, stand on their *hind* legs, and push on each other with their forefeet. The first to fall over loses, though they may fight more times, and the older fox usually wins in the end. The territory a fox settles on may be several miles wide; if food is scarce it may be even wider.

By winter, usually in January, the cycle begins again. Young red foxes will mate for the first time. The young vixen attracts males by her scent. At the same time, older foxes may either seek out their former mate or choose a new mate with whom to bear more young. They may even use the same den as before.

Did You Know . . .

Foxes mark their territory by urinating in various places, leaving a distinct scent that tells other foxes "this area is taken."

There's no playing going on here as two red foxes fight with teeth bared.

In spring, foxes shed their thick coat in clumps in exchange for a lighter one. In the process, they get quite shaggy. This temporarily unkempt look is a small price to pay for the comfort a thinner coat gives them in the coming warm months.

4 Foxes Worldwide

The world is home to an estimated twenty-three species of fox. Of those, ten are called "true foxes," and include the common red fox. Foxes are native to every continent except Antarctica and Australia, but red foxes have lived in Australia since humans introduced them there in the 1800s.

The red fox lives throughout most of North America, from northern Mexico to the Arctic, and in Europe, Asia, and North Africa. The red fox is the largest fox, and the European variety grows bigger than the North American one. The coats of red foxes are not always shades of red, and none are stop-sign red. They are usually red blends such as reddish brown or reddish orange, but can be another color

You can see the dark fur along the back, tail, and legs of this red fox as it dives under the snow to hunt for mice.

31

entirely such as black, silver, gray, or yellow. About a quarter of red foxes are cross, meaning streaked with dark fur down the back and across the shoulders. Regardless of the upper-coat color, fox bellies are usually white or light yellow.

The gray fox lives in the woods and swamps of the United States, Central America, and South America. Their gray coats have patches of red on the ears,

A gray fox stays still among the grass and flowers of Montana.

A close-up photo of an arctic fox lets you see its small, round ears.

neck, and legs. It is the only type of fox known to climb trees. Gray foxes are slightly smaller than North American red foxes. While red foxes are sometimes out during the day, gray foxes rarely are. These two species are the most abundant types of foxes in the United States.

The arctic fox lives along arctic coasts, frequently on tundra or mountainsides and farther north than almost every other land mammal. During mating they take shelter in burrows, some of which are hundreds of years old and may have numerous entrances or exits. The litter size of arctic foxes may be up to fifteen, but is usually seven to eleven kits.

Unlike the pronounced triangular pointed ears of most foxes, the ears of arctic foxes are small and rounded, making them less vulnerable to the cold.

This arctic fox has a blue coat for the winter.

Did You Know . . .

The temperature must drop to -94 degrees Fahrenheit (-70 degrees Celsius) before arctic foxes start to shiver.

For the same reason, their paws are covered with thick fur, even underneath. Their bodies are stockier than foxes that live in warmer climates. In summer, arctic foxes are brown or gray; in winter, they turn either stark white or bluish gray, at which point they are called blue foxes. No other foxes have coats that change color seasonally.

Arctic foxes do not hibernate and may be active day or night. They are largely scavengers and known for traveling great distances. At times, they follow polar bears and feed on the remains of the animals the bears kill. If lemmings are available, they will feed plentifully on them. A portion of their diet may be birds, eggs, or squirrels.

The fennec fox (or desert fox) is the smallest fox. Fennec foxes live in the Sahara and Arabian deserts. They are 9.4 to 15.7 inches (24 to 40 centimeters) long, weigh about 1.5 to 3.5 pounds (.6 to 1.5 kilograms), and are about 8 inches (20.3 centimeters) tall. Relative to body size, the ears of a fennec fox are the largest among foxes. Their coat is cream colored and fluffy, which deflects heat during the day and provides warmth on chilly desert nights. Furry soles prevent their feet from getting burned by the hot desert sand. Fennec foxes sometimes burrow into the sand to stay cool during the day. At night, they hunt insects, small

Large ears appear even larger on the small fennec fox.

lizards, small mammals, and birds. They can jump 2 feet high and 4 feet forward, which helps them catch prey and escape predators.

The kit fox is sometimes called the swift fox, though some scientists believe they are separate species. They are the second smallest foxes, after fennec foxes. They live in the drier parts of western North America, such as the Mojave Desert, occupying burrows in sand dunes or under grass mounds. Their coats are pale gray, tan, or yellow. Their ears contain special hairs that block sand from getting in them. As

An adult swift fox looks as small as the kits of some other fox species.

The large ears of bat-eared foxes help them find the insects they prefer to eat.

one of their names implies, these foxes can move swiftly over short distances and often zigzag when they run. Rather than eat prey where they kill it, kit foxes tend to bring it to their den first.

The bat-eared fox lives in the open grasslands of eastern and southern Africa. Bat-eared foxes can grow to be 28 inches (70 centimeters) long and weigh between 6.6 and 10 pounds (3 to 4.5 kilograms). Their coats are typically yellowish gray, helping them blend into their surroundings in an area that is home to many large predators. Bat-eared foxes resemble red foxes except for their large, cupped ears. These ears help them find food underground. Insects, particularly termites, constitute the bulk of their diet. They also feed on dung beetles, scorpions, spiders, and occasionally small mammals, birds, eggs, or lizards.

Red Fox in the Big City

When people hear the phrase "city animals," many think of pigeons or rats. They may be surprised to learn that red foxes are capable of living in cities—and often do. The resourceful canines are able to find regular shelter and food in an urban environment, all the while keeping their presence there a mystery to the average city dweller. If anyone does see a fox in a city, it is almost always at night when the person may mistake it for a dog.

In cities foxes can often find food more reliably than in the woods or countryside. Trash cans and bags of garbage are on nearly every street, giving foxes an abundant number of sites to rummage

Although this red fox pair probably prefers the New Jersey beach where this photograph was taken, foxes are able to survive in cities as well.

through. Unfortunately, they sometimes eat items from the trash that are not meant to be eaten at all. Foxes also find rodents, insects, and birds in cities, and catch them the same way they would in a secluded field. It does not appear that city living causes foxes to lose their natural instincts.

Cities offer numerous types of shelters for foxes. In the wild, most foxes lead lives undisturbed by people. In cities, it is less likely that a fox can find a resting location that is completely cut off from humans. Some foxes even make themselves comfortable somewhere in a house, unbeknownst to the human inhabitants. Others end up in railway embankments or even more isolated places.

Urban foxes patrol smaller territories since cities are crowded and trash is plentiful. To find reliable sources of food, they may change their territory more often than a rural fox. This can include revisiting former territories to check out the current food situation there. Some foxes change their dens often, too. Because more foxes live in less space in urban areas than in rural ones, rabies and other diseases may spread more easily among city-dwelling foxes.

Did You Know . . .
Foxes can swim, but they do not have a regular need to be in the water.

40

Red foxes can find a place to rest almost anywhere.

Whether they live in cities or the countryside, whether they are red or any other color, whether they have big ears or small, foxes are familiar to people almost everywhere. They are a highly successful species and are unique among the doglike mammals. Though not suitable for pets, foxes sometimes are friendly enough to show themselves to people from a distance. Then, with an expression that may seem sly to some and shy to others, they gracefully scurry off for another meal.

Glossary

breed: To produce and raise young animals.

brush: The tail of a fox.

burrow: A hole created or used by an animal as shelter.

cache: A hidden storage space.

canidae: The family of animals that include dogs, coyotes, wolves, jackals, and foxes.

carrion: The dead body of an animal.

den: A sheltered area where foxes bear young.

dog: A male fox.

domestic: Describes an animal that is tame enough to live, breed, and be comfortable around humans.

endangered: Threatened with dying out.

hind: Describes the rear of something, such as the rear legs of an animal.

kit: A baby fox; also called a cub, pup, or whelp.

litter: A group of babies that a mammal produces at one birthing.

mange: A skin disease transmitted by a mite that causes hair loss.

mite: A tiny animal similar to a spider that attaches to a larger animal and can cause irritation and carry disease.

omnivore: An animal that eats both meat and plants.

parasite: An animal that lives on another animal and feeds off of it.

predator: An animal that hunts and eats other animals.

prey: An animal that is hunted and eaten by other animals.

rabies: A disease caused by a virus that can be fatal to mammals.

solitary: Describes the state of being alone.

tapetum: A reflective surface in the eye of some animals that increases night vision and causes the eye to shine in the dark.

tundra: A region just south of the northern polar ice cap where trees do not grow.

vaccinate: To give an animal an injection to prevent it from getting a disease.

vixen: A female fox.

Find Out More

Books

Arnold, Caroline. *Fox*. New York: William Morrow, 1996.

Barrett, Jalma. *Foxes* (Wild Canines!). Farmington Hills, Michigan: Blackbirch Press, 2000.

Grambo, Rebecca. *The World of the Fox*. San Francisco: Sierra Club Books for Children, 1995.

Henry, J. David. *Red Fox: The Catlike Canine* (Smithsonian Nature Book). Washington, D.C.: Smithsonian Books, 1996.

Matthews, Downs. *Arctic Foxes*. New York: Simon & Schuster Children's Publishing, 1995.

Web Sites

Fox Forest: For Preservation and Education
www.foxforest.org/

Hunt Saboteurs Association
http://hsa.enviroweb.org/hsa.shtml

The OzFoxes Fox Web
www.ozfoxes.com/aafoxes.htm

Index

Page numbers for illustrations are in **boldface**.

About the Author

Marc Tyler Nobleman is an author and cartoonist who has written more than fifty books and drawn forty times as many cartoons. He writes regularly for *Nickelodeon Magazine*, and his cartoons have appeared in the *Wall Street Journal, Barron's,* and *Forbes.*